THE LETTERBOX CAT
& other poems

PAULA GREEN
Illustrated by Myles Lawford

SCHOLASTIC
AUCKLAND SYDNEY NEW YORK LONDON TORONTO
MEXICO CITY NEW DELHI HONG KONG

Paula Green lives on Auckland's west coast. She runs NZ Poetry Box, a blog for children and schools
www.nzpoetrybox.wordpress.com

First published in 2014 by Scholastic New Zealand Limited
Private Bag 94407, Botany, Auckland 2163, New Zealand

Scholastic Australia Pty Limited
PO Box 579, Gosford, NSW 2250, Australia

Text © Paula Green, 2014
Illustrations © Myles Lawford, 2014

ISBN 978-1-77543-223-4

All rights reserved. No part of this publication may be reproduced or transmitted in any form or by any means, electronic, mechanical or digital, including photocopying, recording, storage in any information retrieval system, or otherwise, without prior written permission of the publisher.

National Library of New Zealand Cataloguing-in-Publication Data

Green, Paula, 1955-
The letterbox cat and other poems / by Paula Green ; illustrated by Myles Lawford.
ISBN 978-1-77543-223-4
1. Children's poetry, New Zealand.
[1. Animals—Poetry. 2. New Zealand poetry.]
I. Lawford, Myles. II. Title.
NZ821.2—dc 23

12 11 10 9 8 7 6 5 4 3 2 1   4 5 6 7 8 9 / 1

Illustrations created in Adobe Photoshop with a Wacom tablet

Publishing team: Diana Murray, Lynette Evans, Penny Scown and Frith Hughes
Designer: Dana Brown
Typeset in Garamond Infant ITC Light

Printed in China by RR Donnelley
Scholastic New Zealand's policy, in association with RR Donnelley, is to use papers that are renewable and made efficiently from wood grown in sustainable forests, so as to minimise its environmental footprint.

For Warren and Banu ~ P.G.

To my two sisters, Vittoria and Emma
– the best a brother can have ~ M.L.

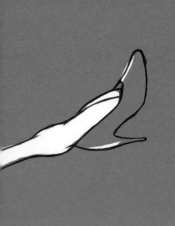

Contents

Shoes	9
A Snail Poem	11
The Rainbow	13
Stars	15
At Sea	17
Kite	18
The Fantail	20
Cat Naps	23
The Letterbox Cat	24
Night Cat	27
The Gargle Bird	29
Rain	30
Winter	33
This Poem	34
The Wood Pigeon	37
Sand	38
When I Am Cold	41
Our Dogcat	42
Snowboarding	44
Popcorn and Nice Ice	46
Hello Spring	49
Leaf	50
Another Leaf	51
Music	53
Fire	55
A Poetry Challenge	56

The Rollercoaster	58
A Bookcat	60
Score!	63
Noses and Toeses	65
A Family of Hungry Mice	67
Autumn and Dandelions	69
Clouds	70
Anifables	72
The Greedy Cat	74
Which Jack?	77
Molly	78
Hiccups	80
Animals	82
Faces	84
The Orange	87
Cloudsville	89
The Library	90
A Slow Sky Tonight	93

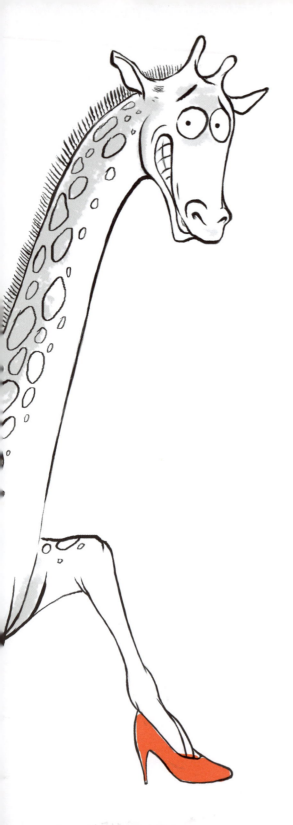

Shoes

Boat shoes

car shoes

bike shoes

goat shoes

giraffe shoes

kite shoes

soap shoes

fluffy shoes

light shoes

rope shoes

tough shoes

MY SHOES!

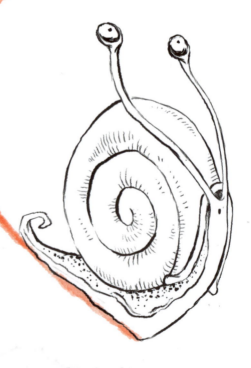

A Snail Poem

A snail slides and slips
down the path
on her silvery snail trail,
with her little house sitting
on her back like a shiny hat.

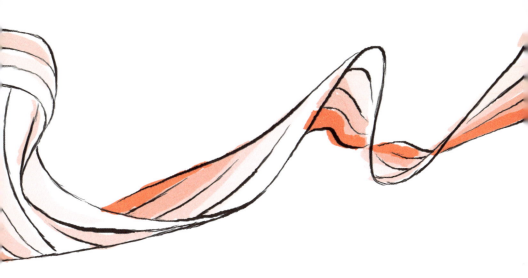

The Rainbow

On a blue day
a rainbow
wraps the sky
with bright ribbons.

Stars

Little holes
in the big black
night blanket
let little bits
of light through,

like drops
of Christmas tinsel
and drips
of glitter paint.

I can see the Southern Cross
and the creamy smudge
of the Milky Way
shining in the night sky.

s
sa
sai
sail
saili
sailin
sailing
sailing b
sailing bo
sailing boa
sailing boat
at sea with me at sea with me
with me at sea with me at sea

At Sea

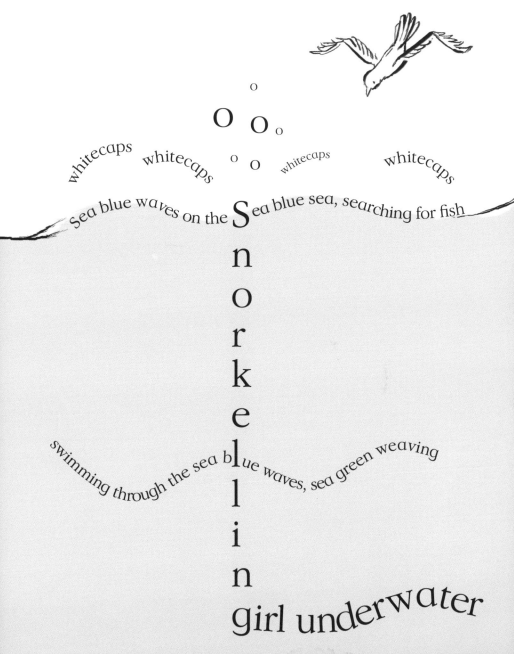

whitecaps   whitecaps   whitecaps   whitecaps

Sea blue waves on the **S**ea blue sea, searching for fish

n
o
r
k
e

swimming through the sea b**l**ue waves, sea green weaving

l
i
n

girl underwater

Kite

MY KITE IS PULLING ME THROUGH THE SKY LIKE A WEE FEATHER SOFT AND BLUE and as I feel the wind in my hair and the sun on my nose I can see my clothes flapping like birds on the line

The Fantail

Jump tail
hop tail
dance tail
skip tail
pop tail
flip tail
boogie tail
woogie tail

fantail!

Cat Naps

If you put your hat
or a box or your coat
or a sock or your cap
or a frock or a boat
on the floor,
our tabby cat
will sleep in it

FOR SURE.

The Letterbox Cat

Our cat climbs
on the top of the letterbox
as if she's waiting
for a letter from
> London
> or Luxembourg
> or Levin,
> or Sydney
> or Samoa
> or Berlin,

but all we get is paper
for our recycling bin.

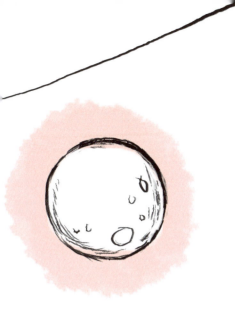

Night Cat

Tw_itching tail
arched back
milky paws,
out
in
the
dark
black
night, my cat
is ready to **pounce**
on moving s h a d o w s.

The Gargle Bird

The tui is a chortle bird,
a chatter bird, a chitter bird,
a chuttle bird.

She wears her feather bow
her snowy bow, her foamy bow,
her white bow,

on her shining black
her sheeny black, her coal black,
her blue black,

in the skinny tree
the spindly tree, the spandly tree,
the cabbage tree,

with her gargle song
her giggle song, her glaggle song,
her tui song.

Rain

The rain
falls on the tin roof
like little horses
showing off their clicketty hooves
pit pit pit pit pit pit pit pit pit pit pit pit pit pit
pit pit pit pit pit pit pit pit pit pit pit pit pit pit.

The rain
taps the glass windows
like little mice
with their scritchity scratchety claws
patter patter patter patter patter patter
patter patter patter patter patter patter.

The rain
drops on my umbrella
like little girls
in tap-dancing shoes
pit patter pit patter pit patter pit patter pit
patter pit patter pit patter pit patter pit.

The rain
falls outside
and I am inside
as snug as a bug
mmmmmmmmmmmm
mmmmmmmmmasleep.

Winter

Some trees lose their leaves in winter.
They look like skinny bald men standing
in the rain and sleet,

but my cat gets so much extra fluff
he waddles down the hallway like
a puffed up duck.

This Poem

This poem feels like climbing a hill

This poem feels like standing STILL

This poem feels like swimming in the sea

This poem feels like it's hurt your KNEE

This poem feels like putting on B R A K E S

This poem feels like eating CAKES eating floating in the sky

This poem feels like asking whywhywhywhy why

The Wood Pigeon

A soupy mix
of sea blue and river green,
with her plump white pillow chest
the wood pigeon flies
flap shlip *flap* shlap

from one tree to the next,
in her hunt for berries
bright red best,
flap shlip *flap* shlap.

Sand

The sand at the beach
is a glorious thing.
You can write a message
with sandy ink.

You can dig a hole
and bury your Dad,
you can look for shells
and find some crabs.

You can bury treasure for someone to find
you can decorate castles ready to climb
you can count the grains in the winking sun

will you reach a million
when the day is done?
You'll get sand in your sandwiches
and sandy toes,
sand in your eyes when the wind blows.

You can fill a bucket
you can dig a moat
you can race along it
and build boats to float.
When the tide comes in
and washes castles away,
the sand will stay
for another beach day.

When I Am Cold

When I am cold
I get goose bumps.

When I am very cold
I get tiger bumps.

When I am very very cold
I get rhinoceros bumps.

When I am very very very cold
I get elephant bumps.

When I am very very very very cold
I get whale bumps.

When I am very very very very very cold
I drink hot chocolate and wear thick socks.

Our Dogcat

Our playful cat
is a dogcat because she
can fetch a toy
and bring it back,

but our dog
is not a catdog.
He barks and yaps
if I put oily fish
in his doggy dish.

Snowboarding

freshly

fresh
falling
snow

Snow white on the mountain top cold as my freezer

snowboarding

snowboarding

snowboarding

freshly   *freshly*

fresh
falling snow

white as lemonade iceblocks white snow so high up

chair lift
chair lift
chair lift

POP CORN

pOp   cOrn

pOp

pOp   pOp   pOp

cOrn   cOrn

pOp

NICE ICE

```
                    orange
                 ooooooooo
                dream straw
           oooooooooooooooooo
            berry ice, raspberry
         ooooooooooooooooooooooo
           cream vanilla slice
         oooooooooooooooooooooo
            lickety split, ice
   i       oooooooooooooooo           i
           cream lips lickety
      c       oooooooooooo              c
   e          goo chocolate chew      e
       c      oooooooooooo              c
   r          hokey pokeyho           r
       e      ooooooooooo             e
              toffee toffeeto
       a      oooooooooo              a
              fudge fudge
              xxxxxxxxx
   m          limelimeli              m
              xxxxxxxx
       m      apricotapr              m
              xxxxxxx
       e      boysenber               e
           l  xxxxx                l
              nice
           t  xxx                  t
       s      x                       s
```

47

Hello Spring

Lambs
daffodils
jandals
jonquils.

Light when you wake,
light when you skate.
Chickens
blossoms
showers
shorts.

Warm in the water,
warm when you walk.

Leaf

The
    big
       orange
           leaf
              in
           the
         shape
        of
      a ★
             falls
         to
        the
          ground
        as
       if
       to
     say
   "Good
       morning
    autumn."

Another Leaf

The
 big
 red
leaf
 in
  the
   shape
  of
   a
    falls
     to
    the
   ground
    as
    if
     to
   say
     "Goodbye
  summer
      weather."

Music

Music that fills my room is like words floating around in the air and I hum and hum and hum *and* I hum and hum and hum sweet notes to lift like a bird

Fire

In the fire
I can see

hot mouths
and hungry acrobats

deadly monsters
and dancing hats

shining eyes
and secret caves

flying fingers
and fiery waves.

A Poetry Challenge

Try writing a poem
with a fox, a whistle and a box.

The fox might hide in the box
while you have a go on the whistle.

The fox might play the whistle
while you hide in the box.

You might hide the whistle
while the fox hides the box.

You might chase the fox
while the whistle chases the box.

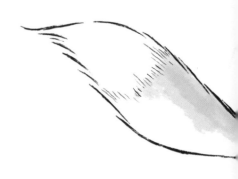

The box might chase you
while the whistle chases the fox.

You might whistle the fox
while the box blows the whistle.

You might put the fox and the whistle
in the box and go feed the chooks.

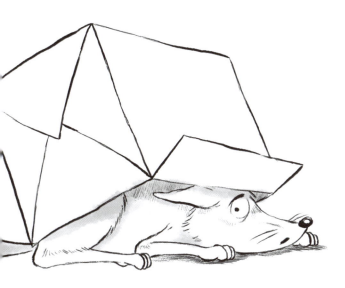

The Rollercoaster

My eyes are streaming. My eyes are streaming at such a speed I need to scream. **Today** I'm on the rollercoaster coasting at such a speed I need to scream. This is fast I laugh and then the speeding thing gets faster and so does my laughter.

terribly terrifying streaming screaming most definitely absolutely awesomely fun CHAIR!

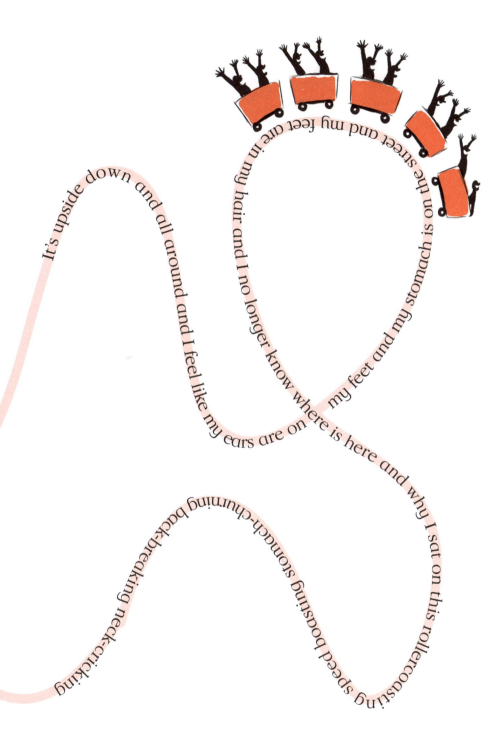

It's upside down and all around and I feel like my ears are on my feet and my stomach is on the street and my feet are in my hair and I no longer know where is here and why I sat on this rollercoasting speed boasting stomach-churning back-breaking neck-cricking

A Bookcat

A bookworm gobbles her way
through books
for breakfast lunch and dinner,
but I am a bookcat.

I like to go hunting
in the mysterious night
and the shining day
of the pages.

I like to shut myself
away in a book
like it's my warm
and cosy cat basket.

Score!

Imagine if you
and your Dad or Mum
could climb into the TV
and see the All Blacks
and the Wallabies play at the park,

and spy rucks and mauls and scrums
spectacularly close tries
forward passes and winning runs.

You could eat hot chips
and puff out hot air
and leap up for the Mexican wave
to the sound of Pacific drums.

At the end of the match
you would climb back
with a signed rugby ball
and a souvenir scarf
to show your rugby chums.

Noses and Toeses

You blow your nose
and wriggle your toes,
but do you wriggle your nose
and blow your toes?

A Family of Hungry Mice

Not much room on a mushroom
for a family of hungry mice.

I wish on a dandelion
for a world at peace.

Autumn and Dandelions

In autumn
the leaves weave
about me
like a

      s ^c r _a p

        p ^a p e r

  s t o r m.

Clouds

The clouds float like marshmallow kisses

Anifables

The porcuswan
is prickly and pale.

The crocodog
chases its tail.

The hippopotamouse
is fond of cheese.

The elephator
dislikes peas.

The cathawk
soars like a kite.

The lioniwi
is awake at night.

If you think these creatures are odd
you should see my fishdog.

The Greedy Cat

The greedy cat
ate cheesy pizza
juicy hamburger
porridge with oats
sardines on toast
spaghetti with clams
eggs and spam

scoff scoff scoff scoff scoff scoff scoff

and then
he went
to sleep
and
sleep
and
sleep

Which Jack?

A Jack in the box

a Jack in his socks

a Jack in the moon

a Jack in tune

a Jack on the grass

a Jack's gone past

a Jack on a camel

a Jack and his flannel

a Jack climbing rocks

a Jack in a box.

Molly

Molly needs swimming lessons
because when she dog paddles
she smash paddles.
Her paws go

CRASH

splash

screech

scrash

like a chomping champing
concrete mixer.

Hiccups

Hic   cup

hic   mug

hic   fork

hic   spoon

hic   stork

hic   bug

hic   STOP!

hic hic hic hic

CUP!

Animals

STRIPYTIGER
STRIPYTIGER
STRIPYTIGER
STRIPYTIGER
STRIPYTIGER
STRIPYTIGER

xsssssssssssnakeinthegrasssssssss

82

TALL
V
 L L
 L L
  L L
  L L
   L
   L
   GIRAFFE
   I   E
   I   E
   I   E
   I   E
   I   E
   I   E
   I   E
   I   E
   I   E
   I   E
   I   E

crocodile IS HUNGRY!
crocodile

Faces

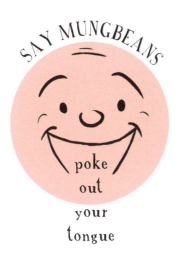

The Orange

I saw little ships instead of pips
on a sea of orange waves.

Cloudsville

Maybe there is a little city
in the clouds where everyone
rollerblades to school
and swims in fluffy swimming pools,
eats cloudyfloss and cloudybuns
and climbs very tall ladders to
pick cloudyplums.

When it's cold, it's puffy mittens
the nana in the cloud is always knitting,
and when it's hot it's ice-cream soda
the cloud granddad is fizzing and floating.

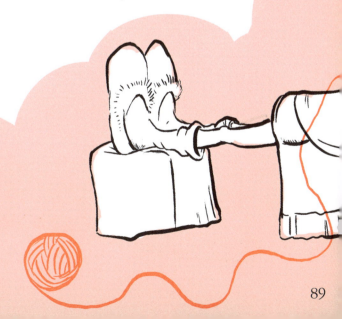

The Library

When I was a girl
the town library was my free ticket
to Mt Everest and stone-age caves
to medieval banquets and magical pools
to Joan of Arc and royal waves
to outer space and why the rain falls.

Now I am older I write poems
to take me to faraway times and
faraway places,
but I still like visiting libraries
for books are like suitcases
waiting to unpack new surprises.

A Slow Sky Tonight

The clouds are moving
across the sky like tiny snails,
the trees whisper tiny secrets
that nobody can hear
and a pink light lights up
the faraway hills.
Dinner is nearly ready.

When words soar through the air
and smack the paper,
somewhere between story and song,
a poem emerges.
— Monica Koster, age 11

I open my ears to let poems come in.
I open my heart to let poems come out.
— Daniel Lovewell, age 5

A poem is not just words,
 it's a creature, wild and untamed.
— Freja Meulengracht-Madsen, age 10

To me, poetry is a way to exhaust ideas
and take things off your mind,
like a train moving forward,
leaving smoke trailing behind it.
— Ewen Wong, age 11